16.00

**JUNIOR
ROOM**

ONE FINE DAY

✦ A Radio Play ✦

WRITTEN BY ELIZABETH VAN STEENWYK
ILLUSTRATED BY BILL FARNSWORTH

ONE FINE DAY

✦ A RADIO PLAY ✦

WRITTEN BY ELIZABETH VAN STEENWYK
ILLUSTRATED BY BILL FARNSWORTH

EERDMANS BOOKS FOR YOUNG READERS
Grand Rapids, Michigan   Cambridge, U.K.

For Brett and the gift of flight he gave his father.
— *E. A. V.*

To my wife, Deborah, and my daughters, Allison and Caitlin.
And a special thanks to my models, Kim Belsan and Jesse Erlich.
— *B. F.*

Text © 2003 by Elizabeth Van Steenwyk
Illustrations © 2003 by Bill Farnsworth
Published in 2003 by Eerdmans Books for Young Readers
An imprint of Wm. B. Eerdmans Publishing Company
255 Jefferson S.E., Grand Rapids, Michigan 49503
P.O. Box 163, Cambridge CB3 9PU U.K.

Manufactured in China

03 04 05 06 07 08 09 10   8 7 6 5 4 3 2 1

Library of Congress Cataloging-in-Publication Data
Van Steenwyk, Elizabeth.
One fine day / written by Elizabeth Van Steenwyk ; illustrated by Bill Farnsworth
p. cm.
Summary: In the form of a radio play, portrays the Wright Brothers' first successful flight.
ISBN 0-8028-5234-3 (hardcover : alk. paper)
1. Wright, Orville, 1871-1948—Juvenile drama. 2. Wright, Wilbur,
1867-1912—Juvenile drama. 3. Aeronautics—Juvenile drama. 4.
Inventors—Juvenile drama. [1. Wright, Orville, 1871-1948—Drama. 2.
Wright, Wilbur, 1867-1912—Drama. 3. Aeronautics—Biography—Drama. 4.
Plays.] I. Farnsworth, Bill. II. Title.
PS3572.A42275 O64 2003
943'.515--dc21
2002009004

The illustrations were painted with oil on linen.
The display type was set in Coppersblack.
The text type was set in Weiss.
Book design by Matthew Van Zomeren

HOW TO MAKE YOUR OWN SOUND EFFECTS

Sound effects can be created from materials you have on hand, and you can be imaginative and creative in trying new things. Here are some suggestions to help you get started.

Wind:
Wind can be created by blowing softly into the microphone. Various degrees of wind can be controlled by off mike sounds or sharp, staccato-like breaths that will resemble sudden gusts of wind. Recording wind outside is another easy way of creating this sound.

Fire:
Vigorous crinkling of paper or aluminum foil near the microphone will create the sound of fire.

Door opening:
Use an actual door in the room, or build a half door, then open and close it at desired time.

Airplane motor:
Use an old-fashioned electric fan for the sound of a motor turning over. Although this sound is not technically accurate, the imagination of the listener will help.

If these suggestions are not possible for you to reproduce, create a class project with several other classmates by recording actual sounds using a tape recorder from school or home. Or, visit a nearby toy store and see what sounds are available in electronic games and toys. Perhaps the owner will let you record some that are appropriate.

Special thanks to
Richard Mawby for his expert assistance with radio scripting, sound effects, and musical suggestions.

Marion Davis Wright for sharing her late husband's reminiscences as a grand-nephew of Orville and Wilbur Wright.

John Sanford, assistant curator at the Special Collections and Archives, Wright State University Libraries, Dayton, Ohio, for reading this manuscript and providing thoughtful advice and assistance.

Music: UP. ESTABLISH, FADE TO BACKGROUND. (SUGGESTED TITLE: "SOMETHING DOING" BY SCOTT JOPLIN, PIANO ROLL)

Narrator I: One hundred years ago, two bicycle mechanics changed the world. In their shop they built, repaired, and sold bicycles, yet they were curious and creative about other methods of transportation as well. Recently they had become especially interested in flying machines. When they were children, their father had given them a small toy that could lift itself into the air. Their serious study and work began in 1896, when, as adults, they read about the experiments of others in the field of flying and studied flight paths of birds.

Music: OUT.

Narrator II: The Wright Brothers built gliders at first, using only nature's power. But they wanted to do more;
go farther, fly higher, and control the machine. They wanted to build a power-driven, heavier-

than-air, controlled-by-man flying machine. They read, they thought, they experimented. Slowly, Wilbur and Orville Wright began to understand the elements of flight, and so they continued to experiment and study until one fine day, all their knowledge came together.

Narrator I: Now, let's go to the beach of Kitty Hawk, North Carolina. It's early in the morning, December 17, 1903.

Narrator II: Wilbur and Orville Wright, spare and lean as wood shavings, lie on unyielding cots in a shack that has little to offer for shelter. They have lived here for about two-and-a-half months while preparing their flying machine for its journey. This is their fourth trip to Kitty Hawk. They first practiced with three gliders, but now, (PAUSE, WITH EMPHASIS) with a motor-powered machine.

Sound: WIND BLOWING, ESTABLISH, THEN DOWN.

Orville: Are you awake, Wilbur?

Wilbur: No chance of sleeping with that wind howling outside.

Orville: I know. And it's a cold wind, too. I can feel it coming through the cracks in the wall. It seems much stronger than the summer winds we've experienced.

Wilbur: Guess we've got the "suitable wind" that stranger spoke about yesterday.

Orville: (LAUGHING) I think he probably meant that 75 miles-per-hour gale that came through here a week ago. Guess he's like most folks who think all we need is wind to get the Flyer off the ground.

Wilbur: At least he didn't say, "If you were meant to fly, God would have given you wings." Remember when that happened?

Orville: (PAUSE, THEN SOFTLY, SERIOUSLY) The wind, Wilbur. I'm concerned. What do you think its rate of velocity is?

Wilbur: Hard to say, but it's brisk. Maybe, if we wait awhile, the wind will die down to suit our needs. Meantime, we can throw some more wood in the stove and cook some breakfast . . .

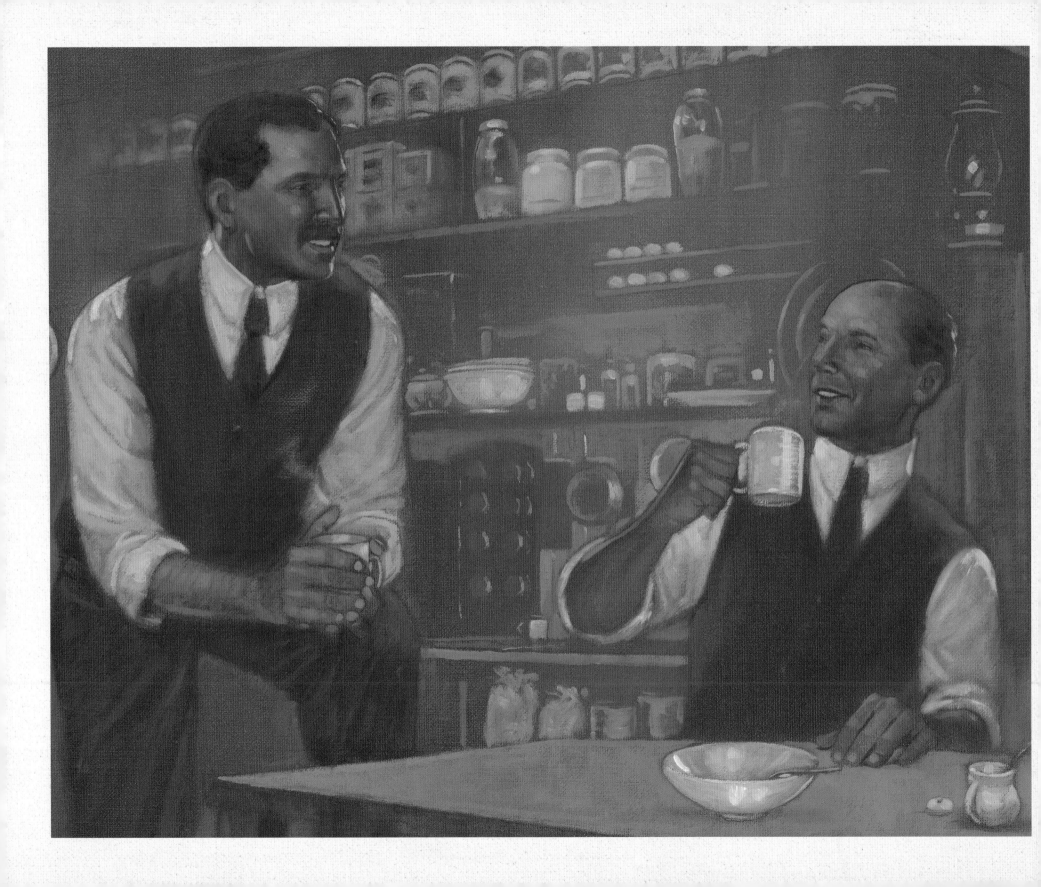

Orville: And, since I'm the cook, guess I'd better get started. Still, I'd rather fly than eat.

Wilbur: You'll get a chance to do both before the day is out, Orville. I'm sure of it.

           PAUSE

Wilbur: Good breakfast, Orville. Your oatmeal didn't have too many lumps this time.

Orville: Or else you're getting used to them. How about a little more coffee?

Wilbur: Just half a cup. Does it seem to you the wind has died down at all?

Orville: Not much. I think we have to make a decision soon. If we want to fly today, we've got a lot to do to get ready. Lay out the track. Hang the signal for the men at the Lifesaving Station . . .

Wilbur: Wonder if they'll come and watch us?

Orville: They came Monday, didn't they?

Wilbur: Yes, and got nothing much to see for their trouble.

Orville: Then we'd better ask them to come back, because we are going to fly today, Wilbur.

Wilbur: Who said so?

Orville: You did.

Wilbur: And about time you listened to me. Seriously, what really surprises me (BREATH) is why flying hasn't happened before. We've talked about that so many times. Look how long people have been staring at the heavens, waiting to imitate the birds, wanting to fly just like them . . .

Orville:	Know why it hasn't happened? All those experimenters before us got the data wrong. How many times did we find numbers that weren't right?
Wilbur:	(INTERRUPTING) Like those air pressure tables we discovered a couple of years ago. Those tables were just plain, flat out wrong. If we hadn't finally noticed . . .
Orville:	(INTERRUPTING) We had to start from scratch and do our own figuring as a result. Maybe nobody's flown yet because nobody bothered to check the data that was available.
Wilbur:	Until we did. It was pretty brash of us to do it though. After all, the man who wrote out the tables is in charge of that museum down in Washington. But it was fun to figure out something nobody else had thought of before. Come on now, Orville. Admit it. It was fun when we straightened out the air pressure tables and got 'em right.
Orville:	Yep. Yep, that was fun.
Wilbur:	And when the Flyer gets off the ground this morning, that's going to be the most fun of all.
Orville:	(PAUSE) Got any doubts, Wilbur? Any doubts at all?
Wilbur:	Not a one. How about you?
Orville:	Never did.
Wilbur:	I think the wind is letting up now. About time we get started.

Sound:	DOOR OPENS. (PAUSE) DOOR CLOSES. WIND IN BACKGROUND.
Wilbur:	Just look at that sky. And those clouds. Ignore that sand, Orville. It's a fine day to fly.
Orville:	And it's my turn, in case you don't remember. We flipped a coin, and you got to fly on Monday.
Wilbur:	Three-and-a-half seconds is all, Orville. That hardly counts. But you go first today. I know that. Now, let's get the track laid over there on that smooth stretch of sand.
Orville:	Let me raise the signal flag for the boys at the Lifesaving Station first. They just might get here in time to give us a hand.
Wilbur:	Good thinking. I'll start hauling stuff out of the shed.
Orville:	Better wait till the last minute to take the Flyer out though. That wind could give us trouble.
Wilbur:	We should have thought of a different name for the machine.
Orville:	Why? Flyer fits it perfectly. All we want it to do is fly.
Wilbur:	But maybe something fancier would have been easier for folks to remember in the future.
Orville:	No, no, I don't think so, Wilbur. We've been calling it Flyer all along. No point in changing its name now.
Wilbur:	Of course, you're right. Smart, too. I hear you take after your older brother.
Orville:	(LAUGHING) Which one? I've got three of them.
Wilbur:	You've got me there, Orville. Grab that end of the track and start lifting.

Sound:	SOUNDS OF EXERTION FOLLOW. SNATCHES OF CONVERSATION: "Bring it over this way." "Take it to the left." "Got it?" "There, that's good." ETC.
Orville:	That should do it, I think.
Wilbur:	Well, I believe we've thought of everything. The machine looks good, the track is nice and straight . . . no bumps that I can see.

Orville: (BLOWS ON HIS HANDS) I think I'll just go inside and warm up a bit before we get started. Never figured on it being this cold.

Sound: DOOR OPENS (PAUSE) DOOR SLAMS. SOUND OF WIND GROWS QUIETER.

Wilbur: Don't forget, it is December.

Orville:	One consolation about that. Don't have to worry about any pesky mosquitoes and black flies. That first summer I thought they were going to bite right through our socks and underwear.
Wilbur:	You know, a week from tomorrow is Christmas. I'd like to wind up things here so we can be back in Dayton with the family for the holidays.
Orville:	We'll make it, 'specially if we fly today. Boy, the fire feels good.
Sound:	FIRE CRACKLING IN STOVE.
Orville:	Smells good, too. Was using the carbide can for a stove your idea or mine?
Wilbur:	Don't remember. I think our ideas have always sort of run together, just like our bank account. If anybody ever asks us, it'll be hard to say who invented what on our motor-powered flying machine.
Orville:	(PAUSE) Say, I think I hear folks outside. Some of the fellas from the Lifesaving Station must have seen the flag and want to watch us try again.
Wilbur:	The folks that live around here don't seem inclined to attend though. They didn't come on Monday, and doesn't look like any of them are coming today.
Orville:	So far, we haven't done anything worth watching. I guess we have to fly first, Wilbur.
Wilbur:	I got a feeling that's about to happen. Come on, January is a cruel month. Let's fly before December gets away from us. Say, let's remember to send Pa a telegram if we succeed.
Orville:	Good idea. Let's go.

Sound:	DOOR OPENS. (PAUSE) WIND SOUNDS LOUDER. DOOR CLOSES.
Orville:	(SHOUTING ABOVE THE WIND) Hi, folks. Glad you could spare some time from the Lifesaving Station. We're about ready to try the Flyer again. If anybody wants to help, grab hold of the wings and hold her down until we're set. Oh, say, Mr. Daniels, would you stand by the camera there on that tripod and click it when the machine reaches the end of the track? My brother and I would appreciate it.
Wilbur:	Orville, time to go. I can't hold this wing down much longer. Climb aboard. (PAUSE) There, looks like you're all set.
Orville:	We've got our wind all right. It wants to do all the work.
Wilbur:	Keep control now, Orville, and let the wind help you, especially when you land.
Orville:	(IMPATIENTLY) All right, all right. I'm starting the motor now, to let it heat up for a few seconds. Hang on.
Wilbur:	Let me know when you're ready.

Sound:	AIRPLANE MOTOR STARTING, THEN RUNNING SMOOTHLY.
Orville:	(CALLING OVER WIND AND MOTOR SOUND) Got to start now, Wilbur. The machine won't hold still any longer.
Wilbur:	I'll run beside you as long as I can keep up. Hang onto your cap so it doesn't get tangled up in the wings.
Orville:	I'm releasing the wire that holds the Flyer to the track. (REALLY EXCITED) Here we go. We're moving forward. It feels good. Steady, real steady.

Wilbur:	(BREATHLESSLY) But you're not moving very fast. What's wrong?
Orville:	The headwind's kicked up. Can't believe it got so strong. Come on, come on, let's go. Faster, let's go faster now. There, we're picking up speed. Here we go. This is wonderful. The wind on my face never felt so good.
Wilbur:	Here comes the end of the track. Here it comes and there you go. Orville, you're off the ground, you're flying! Orville, (SHOUTING NOW) Orville, can you hear me? You're flying!

Orville: (SOFTLY TO HIMSELF) I can't believe that I'm off the ground. I'm in the air, and the Flyer is doing it. No, I'm doing it, too. All that work, all those hours, and now it's happening. Did Mr. Daniels take the picture? Where's Wilbur? He should be here too. How far have I gone? Oh, no, I can't control the front rudder. We should have worked harder on it. It's making me turn too much. The Flyer is turning too much. It's going down, down, but I'm still in control. I can't let the Flyer take over now. Here we go back down to earth. Aaah. That's good. That's nice. The wind is helping me land and the machine is all right and I am too, because I have flown in the air like a bird. Not far, not long, but enough. For now.

Wilbur: (BEGIN OFF MIKE, THEN COME UP TO THE MIKE) Orville, Orville, you flew for twelve seconds. Look, I clocked it.

Orville: (EXCITED) How far did I go? How far? Tell me.

Wilbur: Don't know yet, till I figure it. But, oh, my, you flew right off, Orville. I think our pa's going to be mighty proud of you.

Orville: Proud of both of us, Wilbur. Today, the Wright Brothers flew the first powered machine into the air. Say, I've forgotten. What day is this?

Wilbur: It's Thursday, December 17, 1903, Orville. (BREATH) One fine day for flying.

Narrator I: The Flyer actually flew 120 feet on that first flight, and it flew three more times that day. Then a sudden gust of wind sent the flying machine careening over and over on the sand, and it was damaged to the point that it did not fly again, ever. But the Wright Brothers were satisfied with the results of the day and began to think of how they could improve the machine. Later, they walked four miles to the Kitty Hawk weather station to send a telegram to their father. As they walked, they quietly and surely stepped into history.

Music: UP TO FILL TIME, FADE OUT. (SUGGESTED TITLE: "COME JOSEPHINE IN MY FLYING MACHINE" SUNG BY BILLY MURRAY AND ADA JONES)

Wilbur and Orville Wright's original airplane was on exhibition in Great Britain for more than twenty years. A formal ceremony was held when it was returned to the Smithsonian Institution in Washington, D. C., on December 17, 1948, the forty-fifth anniversary of the first flight. The exhibition label states:

The Original Wright Brothers' aeroplane. The world's first power-driven heavier-than-air machine in which man made free, controlled, and sustained flight. Invented and built by Wilbur and Orville Wright, and flown by them at Kitty Hawk, North Carolina, December 17, 1903. By original, scientific research the Wright Brothers discovered the principles of human flight. As inventors, builders, and flyers they further developed the aeroplane, taught man to fly, and opened the era of aviation.